THE POCKET BOOK OF PANIC

THE POCKET BOOK OF PANIC

Dr. Steven Harris
&
Matt Broadway-Horner

ISBN: 1530327229
ISBN 13: 9781530327225

Dedications

We would both like to dedicate this book to our respective families and partners. Thank you for your unconditional love and support.

Acknowledgments

We would both like to thank our teachers and our patients for contributing towards our knowledge and experience in this subject area.

Contents

About this book

The Pocket Book of Panic was designed to act as a readily accessible and concise guide to help deal with panic attacks. The assumption here is that you have been formally assessed by a medical health practitioner and that you have made an informed decision to try this form of self-help therapy.

Part One of the book presents a summary overview of panic attacks and Part Two presents the techniques. The main focus of this book is on using evidence based techniques, Cognitive Behaviour Therapy and Mindfulness in order to quickly and effectively overcome panic attacks.

At the bottom of each page you will find a space where you can record personal notes, including monitoring your own progress. It is hoped that with commitment to change and daily practice, you will learn to become your own counselor and develop a healthier way of thinking, feeling and acting.

PART 1: Overview of Panic Attacks

Definition of Panic Attacks

You are having a panic attack if you are suddenly experiencing a feeling that something terrible is about to happen to you (impending doom) along with at least four of the following physical and cognitive symptoms: breathing difficulties, racing heart, sweating, difficulty swallowing, difficulty concentrating, dizziness, tingling sensations; you may also feel like you are removed from the situation and that things around you are not real, or that you are losing control.

Panic attacks may also sometimes be associated with agoraphobia which is a fear of being in a situation where there is no easy escape. Panic attacks typically last a few minutes, but may continue for longer; they are not dangerous and do not cause physical harm.

Panic attacks are very common in both men and women, and across all cultures, with one in twenty people having experienced at least one panic attack during their lifetime. Many people experience multiple episodes; termed as a 'panic disorder'.

Notes:

Common Examples of Panic Attacks

People have panic attacks about many different things, from physical symptoms (fainting, vomiting, choking) and conditions (heart attack, stroke, seizures) to fear of losing control or being made to look like a fool.

However, the most common form of panic is 'panic about panic' where the person experiences panic attack symptoms in anticipation of his, or her next panic attack.

Notes:

Causes of Panic Attacks

The exact cause of panic attacks is not known. Anyone can experience a panic attack at any time. Studies involving twins suggest that genetics may play a role and there appears to be a correlation with environmental factors such as stress. The symptoms of panic are identical to the 'fight or flight' response which is a mechanism in the nervous system designed to protect us from danger, such as an intruder. The response involves a surge of adrenaline to prepare us to either fight or to flee. However, during a panic attack there is no real intruder, only a perceived one.

Notes:

Treatment of Panic Attacks

There are many different treatments for panic attacks, ranging from psychological therapies to medication. While certain medications can be very effective in the treatment of panic attacks, they tend to be used more for short-term relief because of potential side effects. Psychological therapies can offer both a short-term and long-term solution. On occasion, both medication and therapy may be used together with a good outcome.

<u>*Notes:*</u>

Medication for Panic Attacks

Medications may be obtained from your GP, mainly for short-term relief. These include beta-blockers, anxiolytics or antidepressants. Beta-blockers such as propranolol work on the heart to slow down the heart rate. Anxiolytics such as alprazolam and antidepressants such as citalopram work on the brain to modify neurotransmitters, such as serotonin, which helps reduce symptoms of panic attacks.

Side effects can range from irritability to sedation and depression. Antidepressants can cause exacerbation of symptoms during the first two weeks of use and may be coupled with an anxiolytic to offset this effect. Taking anxiolytics for more than a few weeks is usually highly addictive.

Notes:

Other Forms of Therapy

There is some scientific evidence to suggest that hypnosis, relaxation and meditation techniques may be helpful in the treatment of panic attacks, especially in conjunction with Cognitive Behaviour Therapy. A naturopathic drug called St Johns Wort has also proven to be of some benefit. However, there is no scientific evidence to show that other remedies and other forms of alternative therapy do much beyond a placebo effect.

Notes:

Diet and Exercise

There is good scientific evidence to show that a well balanced healthy diet and regular exercise can help in the treatment of panic attacks. Try to have regular meals and to avoid sugar, caffeine and alcohol as much as possible. Also avoid illicit drugs like cannabis, amphetamines and cocaine; these act as stimulants. Try to do 30 minutes of moderate aerobic exercise such as cycling, swimming, or fast walking for five days of the week to improve your overall sense of wellbeing.

<u>*Notes:*</u>

Sleep Hygiene

Lack of sleep may contribute to panic attacks. Improve your sleep by practicing sleep hygiene:

- Keep the bedroom cool and use it for sleep and sex only. Avoid watching television in the bedroom.
- Practice going to bed at the same time at night and waking at the same time in the morning. Avoid lie-ins.
- Leave the bedroom if you do not fall asleep within 15 minutes and return when ready to sleep again.

- Have a warm bath 90 minutes before sleep time.
- Exercise regularly, but not too close to bedtime.
- Avoid caffeine in the afternoons.
- Have a cheesy snack, or a glass of milk before sleep; these contain naturally sedating ingredients, tryptophans.

Notes:

Psychological Therapies

There are many psychological therapies available for the treatment of panic attacks. This book focuses on the two main evidence-based scientific therapies: Cognitive Behaviour Therapy (CBT) and Mindfulness.

According to CBT, we tend to feel unhealthy emotions and act in non-constructive ways when we are holding irrational beliefs. Challenging our irrational beliefs and changing them to rational beliefs helps us to experience healthy emotions and to act in constructive ways.

Mindfulness involves the focusing of our attention in an accepting and non-judgemental way on our thoughts, emotions and sensations in the present moment.

Notes:

Healthy versus Unhealthy Emotions

CBT tends to view emotions in terms of the way we think, feel and act. When experiencing an unhealthy emotion such as a panic attack, we tend to exaggerate the threat of the situation, feel overwhelmed by it and act in a way which is not constructive, such as escaping the situation, or avoiding it in future.

When feeling a healthy emotion, such as concern (the healthy counterpart of a panic attack), we can see the situation for what it is, feel appropriately and act in a constructive way toward resolving the situation and/or preventing it from recurring in future.

Notes:

Automatic Thoughts

In a panic situation, automatic thoughts (sayings and images) appear to arise spontaneously and are perceived to be true, even when distorted and inconsistent with reality. According to CBT, an automatic thought can lead to panic symptoms which in turn affect the thought in a 'vicious cycle of panic'.

For example, a minor discomfort in the chest may be perceived as *I am having a heart attack!* This may lead to panic symptoms, such as worsening chest pain, sweating and palpitations, which in turn affect the automatic thought. In

CBT, automatic thoughts are defined as superficial thoughts, appearing to arise from core beliefs.

Notes:

Core Beliefs

According to CBT, it is not so much situations, or events that make us feel and act in certain ways, but rather our underlying set of beliefs which are responsible for our emotions and behavior. These beliefs, referred to as 'core beliefs' are unique to each of us as they are formed by individual combinations of genetics and life experiences. Core beliefs may be 'rational' or 'irrational'; rational beliefs lead to healthy emotions while irrational beliefs lead to unhealthy emotions.

Notes:

Primary Irrational Beliefs

At the very core of emotional disturbance are dogmatic 'musts'. Musts are said to be irrational because they are rigid (they do not allow for what must happen not to occur) and unhelpful (they lead to unhealthy emotions such as panic attacks and impede constructive behavior toward healthy change).

For example: *I must know right now that I will never have another panic attack!* (demand for certainty); *you must never think I'm a fool!* (demand for approval from others); *the world must always be a perfectly comfortable place to be!* (demand for comfort).

Notes:

Secondary Irrational Beliefs

When the demands for certainty, approval, and/or comfort are not met, then we tend to have 'secondary irrational beliefs'. For example, we may feel like it is the end of the world not having certainty about our next panic attack (awfulising); that we cannot stand this and somehow we are falling apart and will never experience future happiness (low frustration tolerance); that we are worthless for demanding certainty in this situation (self-downing).

Secondary irrational beliefs are said to be irrational because they are rigid (they are extreme and inconsistent with reality) and unhelpful (they lead to unhealthy emotions such as panic attacks and also impede constructive behavior toward healthy change).

Notes:

Primary Rational Beliefs

According to CBT, non-dogmatic preferences are at the very core of psychological health. Preferences are said to be rational because they are flexible (they allow for what is not preferred to occur) and helpful (lead to healthy consequences in terms of the way we think, feel and act).

For example: *It would be great to never have another panic attack, but I don't need to know right now* (preference for certainty); *I prefer to not look like a fool, but I do not need the approval of others at all times* (preference for approval); *I would like the world to be a comfortable place, but it does not always have to be* (preference for comfort).

<u>*Notes:*</u>

Secondary Rational Beliefs

When preferences for certainty, approval and/or comfort are not met, then we may have 'secondary rational beliefs'. For example, we may think that it is bad not having certainty about our panic attacks, but that it is not the end of the world (non-awfulising); that it is difficult not knowing, but we can tolerate it and likely experience future happiness (high frustration tolerance); that we are fallible complex human beings, too complex to be rated on the basis of one aspect of demanding certainty (non-downing).

Secondary rational beliefs are said to be rational because they are flexible (they are non-extreme and consistent with reality) and helpful (they lead to healthy consequences in terms of the way we think, feel and act).

Notes:

PART 2: Techniques for Change

Introduction to Techniques

It is recommended that you familiarise yourself with all the techniques (whilst not having a panic attack) in order to find out which one(s) work(s) best for you. Your chosen technique(s) should be challenging, but not overwhelming. As you progress, you may wish to try even more challenging ones.

In the same way that you may train at the gym to improve your physical fitness, it is important to practice your chosen technique(s) as much as possible, in order to strengthen your "emotional muscle". It is highly recommended that you monitor your progress in the form of a Monitoring Chart (Appendix 1).

Notes:

CBT Techniques

Set a Realistic and Achievable Goal

It is important to set a goal which is both realistic and achievable. Of course, it would be great to never experience any form of anxiety again. However, a more realistic and achievable goal would be to experience a healthy emotion, such as concern, in place of an unhealthy emotion such as anxiety and panic. Therefore, consider setting a goal to experience healthy concern in place of panic attacks.

Notes:

Commit Yourself to Change

As human beings, we seek comfort in the familiar, even though at times this can be the very same thing that hurts us. Before you start working toward your goal, it is important to commit yourself to the process of change however uncomfortable. If you are not fully committed, then you will likely encounter resistance along the way.

If you have any doubts about committing yourself to change, then consider doing a 'cost-benefit analysis' to prove to yourself that it is in your interest to work toward your goal of healthy concern. Make a list of the consequences of not changing (short and long-term) as well as the consequences of changing (short and long-term) and compare the two.

Notes:

Take Responsibility for the way you Think, Feel and Act

Once you have set a goal and committed yourself to change, it is important to take responsibility for the way you think, feel and act. In order to prove to yourself that you are responsible, consider an experiment where 100 people were to be placed in your panic situation; would they all react with a panic attack? The answer is clearly not.

In any given situation, different people react differently, each according to his or her unique underlying beliefs about the situation. Given that you are experiencing panic attacks, it is highly probable that you are holding irrational beliefs in the panic situation, and that these are contributing to the way you feel and act.

Notes:

Choose a Specific Example

Start by choosing a specific example (preferably recent, vivid and typical) of when you experienced a panic attack. Choosing a specific example will help you uncover your unique set of irrational beliefs in the panic situation and allow you to apply the techniques necessary for change.

Once you have reached your goal of experiencing healthy concern in your chosen example, you may then apply your new rational philosophy toward other specific examples in your day to day living.

Notes:

Identify and Challenge your Automatic Thought(s)

Referring to your specific example, identify the negative automatic thought(s) (sayings and images) that arose spontaneously in your panic situation. For example: *I'm going to faint!* and challenge this by asking: *What evidence do I have for and against my automatic thought?* and *What is the worst case scenario?*

The evidence against your automatic thought is that it probably never materialised during previous panic attacks and that it can be explained in terms of the 'vicious cycle of panic', rather than something real. The evidence to support your automatic thought is likely to be non-existent.

Even in the worst case scenario, were your automatic thought to become reality, it is likely that you would recover and continue to lead a normal life.

Notes:

Identify your underlying Primary Irrational Belief(s)

Referring to your specific example, ask yourself what primary irrational belief(s) were you placing on yourself at the time you had the panic attack? Were you demanding certainty, approval from others and/or comfort? Panic attack sufferers typically demand certainty about their next panic attack, referred to as 'panic about panic'. For example: *I need to know right now that I'm not going to have another panic attack!*

<u>Notes:</u>

Identify your underlying Secondary Irrational Belief(s)

Referring to your specific example, ask yourself what secondary irrational belief(s) did you place on yourself when your demand for certainty was not met? Were you feeling that the lack of certainty was like the end of the world (awfulising); that you could not stand it (low frustration tolerance); that you were worthless as a result of demanding certainty (self-downing)?

Notes:

Challenge your underlying Must(s)

Challenge your underlying must(s), for example, your demand for certainty, by asking yourself: *What evidence do I have that I must have certainty?* In reality, you have survived without it and chances are that you have experienced many of the joys of life and will continue to do so.

Write examples of positive or happy experiences you have recently had and/or likely to have in future. Now ask yourself: *Is it helpful for me to hold onto the demand for certainty?* Holding onto this irrational belief is clearly unhelpful because it contributes toward panic attacks.

Notes:

Challenge your Awfulising Belief

Apply the same argument to your awfulising belief and ask yourself: *What evidence do I have to support this belief?* The lack of certainty is bad, but there are worse things that could happen to you, for example, a car accident where you experience real physical harm.

Write examples to prove to yourself that there is always something worse that can happen no matter how bad a situation. Therefore, it is bad not having certainty, but not the end of the world. Now ask yourself: *Is it helpful for me to hold an awfulising belief?* Holding this belief is clearly unhelpful because it leads to poor consequences in terms of the way you think, feel and act.

Notes:

Challenge your Low Frustration Tolerance

Apply the same argument to your low frustration tolerance belief and ask yourself: *What evidence do I have to support this belief?* The lack of certainty is difficult to tolerate, but you have survived and furthermore, chances are that you have experienced joy in life and will continue to do so. Now ask yourself: *Is it helpful for me to hold a low frustration tolerance belief?* You will see that holding this belief is unhelpful because it actually contributes to panic attacks.

<u>Notes:</u>

Challenge your Self-Downing Belief

Apply the same argument to your self-downing belief and ask yourself: *What evidence do I have to support this belief?* Demanding certainty about panic attacks represents one negative aspect of you, but you are a fallible, complex human being, made of many aspects, negative and positive; too complex to be rated on the basis of just one aspect. Now ask yourself: *Is it helpful for me to hold this belief?* You will see that holding this belief is unhelpful because it leads to poor consequences in terms of the way you think, feel and act.

Notes:

Adopt your new Primary Rational Belief(s)

Once you have challenged your underlying irrational belief(s), replace them with your new rational one(s):

It would be great to have the certainty that I will never have another panic attack, but I don't need to know this right now (preference for certainty). *I would prefer to never make a fool of myself, but I do not need the approval of others at all times* (preference for approval). *I would like the world to be a comfortable place, but it doesn't always have to be* (preference for comfort).

Notes:

Adopt your new Secondary Rational Belief(s)

Once you have challenged your underlying secondary irrational belief(s), replace them with your new secondary rational belief(s):

It is bad not knowing if I will have another panic attack, but it is not the end of the world in that there are worse things that could happen to me (non-awfulising). *It is difficult to tolerate uncertainty, but I have survived and chances are that I will experience future happiness* (high frustration tolerance). *I am a fallible complex human being, too complex to merit a single global rating of worthlessness based on only one aspect of demanding certainty* (non-downing).

<u>Notes:</u>

Strengthen your conviction in your new Rational Belief(s)

Once you have adopted your new rational belief(s), it is advisable to perform exercises to strengthen your conviction in your new belief(s) so that you can internalise a new rational philosophy. Familiarise yourself with all the exercises and choose the ones which work best for you (and which are challenging, but not overwhelming).

Rate how strongly you believe in your new rational belief(s) from 0 to 100 percent conviction, both before and after each exercise, in order to monitor your progress. The exercises are divided into CBT techniques (cognitive, imagery, emotive and behavioural types) and mindfulness techniques.

Notes:

Teach CBT to a Receptive Friend

Strengthen your conviction in your new rational belief(s) by teaching CBT to a receptive friend. Explain the theory and practice of CBT using your own example of having (or panicking about having) panic attacks. In particular, discuss how you arrived at your new rational philosophy by challenging your underlying irrational belief(s). You may also wish to deepen your understanding of CBT by reading more literature, or attending lectures and seminars.

Notes:

Role Playing

Once you have explained the theory and practice of CBT to a receptive friend, take turns playing the role of your old self with your old irrational belief(s) and your new self with your new rational belief(s). At each turn, try and defend your belief(s) while the other attacks your belief(s) with doubts, reservations, or challenges.

Notes:

ZigZag

The zigzag technique involves playing devil's advocate with yourself. Write down on the left hand side of a page your new rational belief; then move to the right hand side of the page and challenge the belief with doubts, reservations or challenges. Move back to the left side of the page and defend your rational belief by challenging your attack. Repeat these steps from one side of the page to the other (in a zigzag pattern) until all your attacks have been exhausted.

Notes:

Disputing Irrational Beliefs (DIBS)

This structured set of six questions is particularly useful when challenging irrational beliefs:

1. *What irrational belief do I want to question and surrender?*
2. *Can I rationally support this belief?*
3. *What evidence is there to support this belief?*
4. *What evidence is there to go against this belief?*

5. *What are the worst possible things that could happen to me if what I am demanding must not happen actually happens?*
6. *What good things could happen to me if what I am demanding must not happen actually happens?*

<u>*Notes:*</u>

Big I, little i

This exercise is particularly useful if you are holding a self-downing attitude. Reflect on your qualities, both positive and negative and write down as many of these as possible. When complete, have a look at all your different qualities. See for yourself that you are a complex, fallible human being, made of many qualities (Big I) and do not merit a global rating based on a single quality (little i). Remind yourself of this exercise if you put yourself down for thinking, feeling, or acting in a particular way.

<u>Notes:</u>

Rational Coping Self-Statements

The following rational coping self-statements may be repeated as "mindful mantras" throughout the day:

1. *I don't need to know right now whether or not I will have another panic attack. I can live with the discomfort of not knowing.*
2. *I am a fallible, complex human being made of many aspects, both positive and negative. Demanding certainty represents only one aspect of my being.*

3. *It is not great to be demanding certainty about panic attacks, but there are much worse things that could happen to me in life.*
4. *It is not easy living with uncertainty, but I am coping in that I have not fallen apart and chances are that I will experience future happiness.*
5. *While it would be nice to have the approval of others at all times, I can survive without it and even experience happiness.*

Notes:

Rational Emotive Imagery

Rational Emotive Imagery involves recreating the panic situation in as much detail as possible using your imagination. As with all imagery techniques, it is best to sit in a quiet room and to take your time during this exercise.

If, for example, you panic about choking during a meal with others, then recreate the panic scene imagining that you are gradually brought to the panic situation. You may imagine starting at home just thinking about the dinner, then travelling by car, standing outside the restaurant and then sitting at the table inside, talking to the others and then perhaps ordering something small to eat.

At each stage, identify your irrational belief(s) and change these to your new rational one(s). Repeat your new rational belief(s) until your unhealthy anxiety changes to healthy concern, before moving on to the next stage.

Notes:

Coping Imagery

Coping Imagery involves imagining yourself experiencing healthy concern in the panic situation. For example, if you panic about fainting in a public location, then imagine in as much detail as possible how you are coping healthily, in terms of the way you are thinking, feeling and acting.

You may wish to be brought to the panic situation gradually practicing rational coping self-statements (see earlier), experiencing healthy concern and acting constructively at each stage.

<u>Notes:</u>

Time Projection

The aim of this exercise is to show you that your life and the world in general continue after experiencing panic attacks.

Visualise your panic attack and then imagine going forward in time a week, then a month, six months, a year and so on.

At each of these times, consider how your life will go on as usual with healthy concern in place of panic attacks.

<u>Notes:</u>

Surfing the Wave

Surfing the wave involves imagining the panic attack as a large, overwhelming wave and allowing it to diminish in size and potency in much the same way as the wave would as it moves to shore.

Imagine yourself in the panic situation and passively observe the wave of anxiety as it levels to healthy concern.

Notes:

Traffic Exercise

The aim of this exercise is to allow your negative automatic thought(s) to pass by without engaging them in any shape, or form, thereby preventing the vicious cycle of panic.

Imagine yourself standing on the side of a busy highway observing traffic, where each car represents a thought, such as a negative automatic thought. Rather than trying to stop each car and maneuver it (in much the same way that you would engage each of your automatic thoughts), practice being a passive observer allowing each car (or automatic thought) to pass by.

Notes:

Humorous Exaggeration

Applying humorous exaggeration to panic attacks can help restore perspective to an already exaggerated thought. For example, the automatic thought *I'm having a fit* may be substituted with *I'm having a fit the size of an earthquake!* or *I'm about to be sick* with *I'm going to throw up my liver!*

Write down humorous exaggerations of your automatic thoughts and use these when experiencing the latter.

Notes:

Therapist Self-Disclosure

I, Dr. Steven Harris, used to suffer panic attacks whilst working as an intern in hospital. During lunch hours with colleagues, I used to worry that I would choke on my food and be made to look like a fool in front of them. As a result, I ate very little lunch and frequently excused myself to the toilet in order to regain composure.

Through CBT, I identified my underlying demands for certainty and approval from others. With practice, I was able to adopt a rational philosophy and experience healthy concern in place of panic attacks.

Notes:

Shame Attacking Exercise

During a shame attacking exercise, you are encouraged to perform a shameful task while practicing self-acceptance.

The tasks should be performed in public places in front of others you do not know and may involve something weird, or unusual, but not in any way illegal, or dangerous. Examples include walking a banana on a leash in place of a dog, or standing up to announce tube stations on a train as it arrives at each one.

It is imperative that during each task you practice self-acceptance; that you are a fallible, complex human being made of many aspects and that performing the task represents only one behavioural aspect of you rather than the whole.

Notes:

Controlled Breathing

Controlled breathing involves breathing through the nose and moving the tummy rather than chest (abdominal breathing). Regular practice will help to regulate breathing and reduce panic symptoms. Repeat the following steps for two minutes at a time, five times daily:

1. Breathe in slowly and fully through the nose counting 3 seconds (while the tummy gently moves out).
2. Breathe out slowly and fully through the nose counting 5

seconds (while the tummy gently moves in).

Notes:

Progressive Muscular Relaxation

Find a quiet place to lie down and practice Progressive Muscular Relaxation (PMR) twice daily so that you learn to recognize and let go of tension in your muscles.

For each of the muscle groups listed below, tense your muscles for 5 seconds and relax for 10 seconds; then repeat. Practice Controlled Breathing (previous section) during the relaxation phase as you feel the tension leaving your muscles.

Feet – pull toes back and apart
Calves – point toes toward head
Thighs – point toes away from head and push
Buttocks – clench together
Abdomen (tummy) – pull in like being punched
Back – arch fully
Shoulders and Neck – shrug together while arching neck
Arms and Hands – stretch wide apart
Face – shut eyes tightly and clench jaw
Whole Body – tense all muscle groups together

Notes:

Systematic Desensitization

Systematic desensitization involves gradually exposing yourself to the panic situation, either imagining the steps, or actually carrying them out while practicing relaxation techniques at each step.

Write down a hierarchy of panic, from feeling concerned to experiencing a full blown panic attack. For example, if you tend to panic on the tube, then you may use your imagination, or actually start by sitting at home, followed by standing outside your house, then standing 20 meters from a tube station, 10 meters,

5 meters, waiting for the train, sitting inside the train for one station, two stations, etc.

At each step, practice controlled breathing, progressive muscular relaxation, or mindful meditation until your feeling of panic changes to healthy concern.

Notes:

Flooding

Flooding refers to placing yourself directly into the panic situation and staying there until your panic attack passes. The aim is to confront your fears head on, so that you may readily gain control over them. This exercise can be very effective, however, you may feel it is too overwhelming for you. If this is the case, then consider practicing some of the imagery techniques before moving onto this one.

Notes:

Non-Panicky Twin

The non-panicky twin is the part of you who does not suffer panic attacks and experiences healthy type emotions in all situations. Make a list of how your non-panicky twin would think, feel and act in your panic situation. When a panic attack arises, try follow this list, however uncomfortable, to become more like your non-panicky twin.

Notes:

Mindfulness Techniques

Raisin Exercise

The raisin exercise will help you understand the process of mindfulness, before extending the skill to other areas of your life. At each step, be aware and present while gently acknowledging and accepting any unwanted thoughts, feelings, and bodily sensations.

1. Begin by placing a raisin in the palm of your hand and look at it, with a sense of curiosity and awe, as if for the first time. Examine its size, shape, edges, folds, colour, areas of light and darkness.

2. Touch the raisin with your fingers exploring its size, shape and texture.
3. Hold the raisin under your nose and smell its fragrance.
4. Gently place the raisin on your tongue (without chewing) and notice the feel and taste.
5. Start slowly and gently chewing the raisin and note the sensations, textures, tastes and smells. Finally, allow yourself to swallow the raisin and notice how that feels.

Notes:

Mindful Breathing

The primary focus in all forms of mindful meditation is the breathing, which will help you feel more balanced and relaxed. Practice the following steps daily:

1. Sit on a chair in an upright comfortable position.
2. Close your eyes and bring your attention to your belly as it moves out with inspiration (breathing in) and in with expiration (breathing out).

3. When your mind wanders, then gently bring it back to your breath.
4. After a few minutes, gently stop the exercise, open your eyes and continue to be mindful with your daily activities.

Notes:

The Body Scan

This exercise will help you bring your attention back to the sensations of your body to feel and acknowledge that which is present, both physically and mentally. You can practice the body scan daily for only a few minutes at a time, or take up to half an hour to benefit further.

The body scan may be exercised in an upright seating position, or lying down. Focus on one part of the body at a time. At each stage acknowledge your thoughts and feelings, allowing them to be and to run their course.

Start from the feet, then legs, thighs, hips (one side at a time), then move on to the pelvis, abdomen, back (lower, middle, upper), chest, then hands, forearms, upper arms, shoulders (one side at a time), then move on to the neck, jaw, mouth, cheeks, ears, eyes, forehead and temples, top and back of the head.

Finally, feel the body as a whole from head to toe, rising on inhalation and falling on exhalation. As before, be aware and present.

Notes:

Mindful Listening

Mindful listening involves focusing on what the other person is saying as well as his, or her gestures, without interrupting, judging, refuting, or discounting.

If your mind wanders during the process, then slow down, breathe and gently bring your focus back to what the other person is saying.

Pause before responding to introduce a sense of space and calm and develop empathy (both toward yourself and the other person) with a receptive attitude rather than a defensive one.

Notes:

Mindful Mind States

Be mindful of the transient nature of thoughts and emotions. Learn to take a back seat and experience the coming and going of panic attacks like stormy weather. Think of your mind as having a mind of its own and allow it do as it wishes in the knowledge that all mind states are transient.

Notes:

Choiceless Awareness

Be aware of whatever is arising in the present (thoughts, emotions, physical sensations) and become the moment to moment changing experience that is life.

Be mindful of the transient nature of all things in life and allow panic attacks to arise and pass without interference.

Notes:

S.T.O.P

This exercise will help stop a panic attack as it arises. Follow the steps of the acronym S.T.O.P:

Stop for a moment.
Take a deep breath using your belly.
Observe, acknowledge and allow for the thoughts and feelings you have in the present moment.
Proceed with your day and be present with all that is around you.

<u>Notes:</u>

R.A.I.N

This is a self-inquiry exercise which can help you gain insight into the nature of your panic attacks before disengaging them. Practice the following steps of the acronym:

Recognise the feeling of panic.
Allow it to be present.
Investigate the different aspects of your panic attack, in terms of how you are thinking and feeling.

Non-identify with the panic attack and disengage.

Notes:

Sitting Meditation

Sitting meditation combines some of the previous practices to deepen your understanding of change and the transient nature of all things, including panic attacks. Sit comfortably in an upright position and practice each of the following stages for 2-5 minutes at a time, before gently shifting to the next one.

1. Mindfulness of breathing - Be aware of how each breath is different to the one before.

2. Mindfulness of sensations - Feel the changing nature of bodily sensations.
3. Mindfulness of sounds - Listen to the changing sounds around you.
4. Mindfulness of mind states - Be aware of your own changing thoughts and emotions.
5. Choiceless awareness - Be mindful of whatever arises in the present moment.
6. Finally, gently come back to the breath, feeling your body as a whole, from head to toe, rising on inhalation and falling on exhalation.

Notes:

Walking Meditation

Walking meditation allows you to meditate while being active. Practice the following steps, preferably outdoors for 20 minutes at a time:

1. Start by standing still and practice mindful breathing for a few minutes.
2. Shift your attention to your body as you become aware of bodily sensations.
3. Begin walking at a relaxed and normal pace. Gradually scan all parts of your body (starting with

your feet) and let go of any tension. If the mind wanders, then gently bring back attention to bodily sensations.

4. Practice choiceless awareness and be mindful of whatever arises in the present moment.
5. Slowly come to a natural stop and gently return your awareness to the breath, feeling your body connected as a whole.

Notes:

Loving-Kindness Meditation (toward Self)

Loving-kindness meditation will allow you to open your heart to love and compassion toward yourself, others and beyond. Simply acknowledge any unhealthy feelings which may arise during the process.

Find a quiet place and sit upright on a chair. Begin by bringing awareness to your body and mind and acknowledge all that is present. Slowly focus your attention to awareness of breath as you breathe in and out using your belly.

After a few minutes, slowly bring your attention into your heart area and feel the boundless love of the universe which extends to all things, both living and non-living.

Feel the love and compassion you have in your heart toward yourself and allow the loving-kindness to sink into your whole body and being. It may be helpful to reflect upon the following phrases: *May I be safe. May I be healthy. May I have ease of body and mind. May I be at peace.*

<u>Notes:</u>

Loving-Kindness Meditation (beyond Self)

After you have spent a few minutes absorbing loving-kindness into your being, extend the same to each of the following in turn: all those near and dear to you, those who have inspired you, acquaintances and strangers, those who give you difficulty, all things living and nonliving on this earth. Finally, extend loving kindness beyond the earth to all corners of the universe.

Spend a few minutes on each of the above and then gently return to the breath, feeling your entire body rising on inhalation and falling on exhalation. Feel your body connected and whole to both yourself, others, the world and the universe.

Notes:

Breathing Space Meditation

This meditation may be practiced over just 3 minutes, or longer if desired to help you be mindful during the day.

1. Sit down on a chair in the upright position.
2. Gently bring your attention to each of the following in turn: your physical sensations, your emotions and your thoughts.
3. Focus your attention to your breathing and practice mindful breathing.

4. Open up your awareness to your whole body and allow space for all sensations (including breathing) to just be there. Be present and mindful.

Notes:

Grounding Meditation

This meditation will help you feel centred and grounded:

1. Sit down on a chair in the upright position with your feet firmly grounded on the floor.
2. Feel the physical sensation of your feet on the floor and the weight of your body on the chair.
3. Practice mindful breathing, feeling your body becoming heavier with expiration (breathing out) and your feet becoming more rooted to the earth.

4. If your mind wanders, then gently bring back your attention to your bodily sensations.
5. After a few minutes, gently end the exercise and continue your daily activities with mindful awareness.

Notes:

Dealing with Obstacles to Change

If you are finding that having worked through CBT and mindfulness exercises, you are making little progress, then you may have a resistance to change. There may be a number of reasons for this:

1. You hold a low frustration tolerance (LFT) belief that *I should not have to work so hard to achieve change.*

   Challenge your LFT belief and develop a high frustration

tolerance that *I can tolerate working harder to achieve change.*

2. You have achieved intellectual insight understanding the process, but not emotional insight where you internalise and live by the philosophy.

   Identify what is stopping you from practicing a rational, accepting philosophy and challenge these ideas to achieve change.

3. You may feel uncomfortable and unnatural with the change itself and believe that *this is not me.*

   Identify and challenge your underlying demand for comfort and accept that change can feel uncomfortable.

<u>Notes:</u>

Maintain and Enhance your Gains

It is normal during the process of change to experience setbacks and gains:

1. Accept setbacks as normal and remind yourself that you are a complex fallible human being, too complex to be rated on the basis of a setback.
2. Develop emotional insight and live by a rational and accepting philosophy in dealing with small daily examples as they arise.

3. Practice mindful living as a way of life and meditate regularly as part of your daily routine.
4. Ensure you keep physically fit and healthy. Remember that 'fit body equals fit mind.'
5. Set goals which are realistic and achievable, but do not pursue them dogmatically and allow for failure.

Notes:

When to Seek more Help

While self-help therapy can be highly effective, it is worth visiting your General Practitioner (GP) on a regular basis (to be decided with your GP) to monitor your progress and decide if more help is needed.

You should visit your GP immediately, if you notice any of the following:

1. Feeling actively suicidal.
2. Feeling a rapid decline in your condition with worsening symptoms.

Appendix

PANIC ATTACK MONITORING DIARY (HEADINGS)

<u>Date/Time:</u>

<u>Panic Situation:</u>

<u>Panic Level (0-10):</u>

<u>Unhelpful Thoughts or Images:</u>

Coping Technique:

New Helpful Thoughts or Images:

Panic Level (0-10):

References

Altman, D. (2011) *One Minute Mindfulness.* Novato, California: New World Library.

Beck, A.T. (1976) *Cognitive Therapy and the Emotional Disorders.* New York: International Universities Press

Broadway-Horner, M. (2015) *Managing Anxiety using Mindfulness based*

Cognitive Therapy. Seattle, Washington: Mary Beatrice Publishing.

Carver, C.S. & Scheier, M.F. (2001) *On the Structure of Behavioural Self-Regulation. In Boekaets M., Pintrich, P.R. and Zeidner, M. (Eds), Handbook of Self Regulation: Theory, Research, Applications*. San Diago: Academic Press.

Dryden, W. (Ed). (1999) *Rational Emotive Behavioural Counselling in Action*. London: Sage.

Ellis, A. (1998) *How to Control your Anxiety before It Controls you*. New York: Kensington Publishing Corp.

Harris, S., Davies, M.F. and Dryden, W. (2006) *An Experimental Test of a*

Core REBT Hypothesis: Evidence that Irrational Beliefs lead to Physiological as well as Psychological Arousal. Journal of Rational Emotive & Cognitive-Behaviour Therapy, 24(2): 101-110.

Stahl, B., Millstine, W. (2013) *Calming the Rush of Panic.* Oakland, California: New Harbinger Publications.

DR. STEVEN HARRIS

Dr. Steven Harris completed his medical studies in Johannesburg, South Africa in 1997. He then moved to the UK where he worked as a GP in north London for over 10 years. During this time he developed a special interest in mental health and completed his MSc in Cognitive Behaviour Therapy at Goldsmiths College, University of London, in 2005. He was one of the original GPs to offer CBT on the NHS and worked as a GP lead and consultant for IAPT (Increasing Access to Psychological Therapies).

MATT BROADWAY-HORNER

Matt Broadway-Horner is a registered psychotherapist, scientist and nurse. He is the director of Clinical and Wellbeing Services at CBT in the City Clinics. He was first trained in CBT during his post-graduate years at St George's, University of London in 2001. He later completed his master's degree in CBT at Goldsmiths College, University of London, in 2005. As a senior lecturer he was one of the first to train the first generation of IAPT CBT therapists as part of the UK government initiative from 2008 – 2013.

Made in the USA
Charleston, SC
13 May 2016